Can You Be
A Freelance Writer?
Yes, You Can!

Best Wishes!
Julie Scott

Copyright 2013 by Julie Scott
Worcester, MA, USA
Worldwide Rights Reserved.

Published on CreateSpace

Formatted by eBooksMade4You

* * *

All rights reserved. Without limiting the rights under copyright reserved above, no part of this publication may be reproduced, stored in or introduced into a retrieval system, or transmitted, in any form, or by any means (electronic, mechanical, photocopying, recording, or otherwise) without the prior written permission of both the copyright owner and the above publisher of this book.

CreateSpace Edition License Notes

This eBook is licensed for your personal enjoyment only. This eBook may not be re-sold or given away to other people. If you would like to share this book with another person, please purchase an additional copy for each person you share it with. Thank you for respecting the author's work.

* * *

# Contents

## What Is a Freelance Writer?
Pros and Cons
Work Rules
Your Cup of Tea
Pay Your Dues
Be an Interactive Member
Make Profitable Choices
Professional Organizations
Exercises

## Dreams, Goals and Successes
What You Can Write
Technicalities
Newbie v. Seasoned Writers
Exercise

## Mechanics behind Written Information
Saga of the Contraction
Oxford Comma
Then and Than
Your Audience
Key of Three
Semicolons and Compound Sentences
Some Income Statistics
Desktop References
Search for Your First Project
Exercises

# What is a Freelance Writer?

Writers specialize in areas emphasizing their strengths and skills. Some are news journalists, human interest writers, photojournalists, travel writers, editorialists, financial specialists, fiction writers, bloggers, novelists and informational content writers. News organizations, trade publications, feature magazines or other specialty publications hire staff writers.

Then, there are the freelancers. They work alone and tend to write on speculation. Clients come to them with unique writing projects or webmasters find them online. When the writer works online to fill a need, they are web content writers, bloggers or informational writers.

## Pros and Cons

Freelancing has its pros and cons. A freelance writer must be good at time and cost management. Keeping the books straight and accounting for income and expenses is just as important as doing the writing. It is vital to track time spent on each project and the cost to a client.

Writing is a lonesome profession. If you have time on your hands, the skills to write well and the desire to succeed then yes, you can be a freelance writer.

## Work Rules

There is no dress code to follow and deadlines are unique to each client. The writer determines those deadlines by the size and intensity of the project. Once in place, the work load determines the job schedule for a writer who agrees with the client to set and honor that schedule.

The other side of the coin is not a rosy picture. A freelancer has a lonesome lifestyle by virtue of the demands of this career choice, even though production under these circumstances is top notch. They face rejections or revisions and must take on writing that is less than inspirational for them – in order to pay the bills.

## Your Cup of Tea

Each person is unique and this includes writers, too. A good writer is also a reader, especially reading works that relate to the field of writing or to another writer's work. It is the best way to see exactly what writing will sell.

With an interest in a certain style of writing, you only need some knowledge or credentials to thrive with your choice. Courses, seminars and workshops do pop up seasonally as conferences for writers. Sometimes, they are pricey if held in inspirational environments. Never overlook the grants that are available to allow writers to be present.

## Pay Your Dues

Every profession and trade career has an arm of support such as a membership group, professional organization or an association for workers in the field. Writers have a few of their own as well including newsletters and magazines for members to gain perspective from behind-the-scenes and in the field. For writers, a professional association will often open new markets when existing ones are no longer available.

Find the groups that are most beneficial to you as a writer. LinkedIn is a major location for writers to interact and Facebook is a close contender. The social media outlets are free and attract seasoned professionals as well as those who are new to the field.

## Be an Interactive Member

This is a very important concept. To profit from any membership, it is incumbent upon you to give as much or more than you take away. Members of a group may receive access to certain benefits. These could include group health insurance, financial aid in times that are overwhelming: illness, loss of income or a family emergency.

Professional groups offer social contacts with like-minded individuals. When you attend a meeting or conference, you should always take away feelings of camaraderie and make it a desire to be present at the next one. The friendships are important to the growth and development of your writing and speaking.

## Making Profitable Choices

Start with a group that offers you support and advancement with your career. This is so intensely important. Gather information about organizations you are considering. Go "free" before spreading your wings to annual membership dues.

Annual meetings are informational and might be costly. If you can be present … go. Be an active member and accept various positions of leadership. Help to set atmosphere and agenda for the coming year.

## Professional Associations

If courses, conferences, author meet-n-greets, book signings are available, be there. This is a partial list of some groups and organizations to consider:

- American Crime Writers League – $25 annual dues
- American Society of Journalists and Authors – $210 annual dues
- American Writers & Artists Inc -
- Cassell Network of Writers –

- Editorial Freelancers Association – $145 annual dues

- Garden Writers Association – $85 annual dues

- Mystery Writers of America – $95 annual dues

- National Association of Independent Writers and Editors - $99 online only

- National Writers Association – $85 annual dues

- National Writers Union – range from $120-$340 annual dues

- PEN American Center – $125 annual dues

- Society of Children's Writers and Illustrators – $85 annual dues

- Society of Professional Journalists – $75 annual dues

A more inclusive list of Professional Associations for Writers is available online.

~~~~~~~~~~~~~~~~~~~~~~~~~~~~~~~~~~~~~~~

Exercises:

1) Use a separate paper to make a list of your skills, hobbies, interests and abilities. Include everything.

2) How many items on your list are relative matches? (Like tomatoes? Like gardening? Write about growing tomatoes.)

3) What type of writing would best express your passion for those matches on your list?

4) Which professional organization do you think would be most helpful to you as you begin freelance writing?

# Dreams, Goals and Successes

Success is all in your head. Execution is in your gut. If you can dream it, you can achieve it. Is writing a good fit for you? Find out by answering these few questions:

- Are you at home doing unproductive activities daily?
- Are you paying bills with money that does not exist?
- Can you write a letter in good English to send to a friend?
- Do you have a pressing need to increase your income?
- Can you identify your strongest skills and fondest hobbies?
- Do you know how much more cash you need per month?
- Can you work at home to earn the extra money?
- Are you willing to persist in your efforts to earn that cash?
- What do you know that could help you to earn money by writing?

## What You Can Write

Writers are unique individuals. Many avenues are open to everyone, which makes specialization easy. If you enjoy casual conversation, consider blogging for cash. Perhaps you are a more factual person, which means you might be the next fine technical writer.

Start with your own knowledgebase about life, pets, family, hobbies, passions and activities as you grow into a writer:

- Specialty blogs
- Feature articles
- Product reviews
- Web content
- Sales copy
- Editorials
- Fiction Stories
- Financial Writing
- Grant writing
- Letter Writing
- News Writing
- Report Writing
- Sports Writing

- Technical Writing
- Travel Writing
- White paper Writing

## Technicalities

It is time to evaluate your situation to determine if you are on the right track. You must make a coherent sentence from a group of words. Not everyone can do this.

Words are the tools of this career and they often get lost in the fascination of the writer's lifestyle. Concise communication makes a good writer - a fascinating story makes a great writer. Writing is engaging when it is easy to read.

Expert and dynamic use of spelling, punctuation and grammar are keys to your communication skills. Spell, punctuate and use words correctly so that readers will focus on the message rather than its delivery.

## Newbie v. Seasoned Writers

New writers tend to accept assignments where the earnings are meager. Those writers who are able to accept complex assignments receive a much higher income. Writers writing for other writers gain income plus a loyal following for their efforts.

Authors who write for writers include:

- Robert Bly. [How to Write and Sell Simple Information for Fun and Profit.](#)
- Peter Browerman. The Well-Fed Writer.
- I. J. Schecter. 102 Ways to Earn Money Writing 1500 Words or Less.
- Robert Bly. [The Copywriter's Handbook](#).
- Maria Veloso. Web Copy That Sells.
- Ashleigh Jensen. Writing for Cash: Making Money as a Freelance Writer in 2013.

Serious writers often seek advice or mentoring from these authors and own one or more hardcopy titles for reference.

Other valuable titles are available as downloads:

- Angela Booth. Writing for the Web.
- Julie Scott. [Directory of Paying Markets for Freelance Writers](#).
- Andrew Crofts. The Freelance Writer's Handbook.
- Robert Bly. Getting Started as a Freelance Writer.
- Lucy Parker. How to Start a Home-Based Writing Business.

- Jack Adler. [Make Steady Money as a Travel Writer – Without Traveling](#).

~~~~~~~~~~~~~~~~~~~~~~~~~~~~~~~~~~~~~~

Exercise:

On a separate sheet of paper, select the writing style(s) you have the most interest in pursuing. Explain why those choices fit you perfectly.

# Mechanics behind Written Information

Let us begin with a golden rule of information writing. Do not **freely** use contractions. They have the same effect as using slang in research reports. However, when you must use a contraction, be sure it is the correct choice for your sentence.

## Saga of the Contraction

Excellent command of the English language is very important to the success of any writer. It includes the correct use of spelling, punctuation and various parts of speech – such as those aforementioned contractions. Readers want to absorb information without struggling with words. They will miss your message if interpretation or translation becomes a consistent requirement.

Contractions seem to be the bane of a writer's existence. They bring two words together and a writer should know if the choice is correct. Read the sentence out loud and say each part of the contraction as if it was two full words. Here are some contractions with the words they represent:

| | | |
|---|---|---|
| Aren't | = | Are not |
| Can't | = | Cannot |
| Couldn't | = | Could not |
| Don't | = | Do not |

Isn't = Is not

Shouldn't = Should not

You're = You are

## Oxford Comma

Those who are using American English will find great debates about the Oxford comma. The consensus is that it would be better to re-write the sentence and avoid the need for this extra comma. To learn more about Oxford commas, refer to [The Associated Press Guide to Punctuation](#) by Rene Cappon. This comma impacts your writing when listing items within a sentence.

## Then and Than

Contractions and commas are not alone on the list of writing stumbling blocks. A few homonyms and synonyms often get in the way. Word pairs that are often used incorrectly are "then" and "than".

If you pronounce each of them correctly, you should not have a problem using each one. "Then" is an indicator of time differentiating between before and after. "Than" makes a comparison between objects that differ in size, shape, distance, height, weight or depth.

## Your Audience

Does your audience read hard copy books, need a dose of instant gratification by downloading a PDF or do they use an eReader? Maybe you have an audience that uses all three. Your best decision is to format writing for readers with electronic devices.

If you decide to write for the web, the writing must be crisp, concise writing. Online visitors are scanners with short attention spans. Their eyes go down the center of a page looking for keywords and they thrive on plenty of white space on a page.

## Key of Three

Remembering the "Key of Three" when you are making a page "reader ready" will also make it more readable. The first paragraph is an overview of the article in three short sentences.

Following the introductory paragraph, a 500-word article should have a maximum of three subheadings to break up the information. After the introductory paragraph, a subheading follows with a couple of paragraphs.

A paragraph is three sentences and 50-65 words. No sentence should require more than 18 words. Follow this format and the content will look good and be easy to read.

## Semicolons and Compound Sentences

Run-on sentences make a paragraph difficult to read. When you reach a point where the semicolon would normally separate two complete thoughts, use a period instead.

Semicolons separate the compound sentence, which should not be necessary online. Those semicolons make sentences much too long and distracting for online readers.

## Desktop References

These are just a few thoughts about mechanics of using words. A writer should own the hard copy of some great desktop references. One reference I highly recommend is [The Associated Press Guide to Punctuation](#) by Rene Cappon, which is a very useful tool.

Other desktop guides are available for various styles (APA, MLA, Harvard, Chicago and Turabian) online as well as brick-and-mortar bookstores. It is wise to keep at least one guide nearby when you sit down to write. Most freelancers expect to use AP or APA styles for web writing on assignment.

## Some Income Statistics

Writers who enter the mainstream workplace need a Bachelor's Degree to begin working. Most of the activities in a writer's job description will come from on-the-job training to conform to employer expectations. However, freelance writers tend to be part time workers and do not always have – nor do they need - a degree in anything.

The [2012 report](#) from the Bureau of Labor Statistics (BLS) of the United States government indicates the median annual income for workplace writers is $54,210. This means that 50% of the employed writers made less than that and the other 50% made more. Note that freelancers engage in web content writing for internet sites or blogs and they are not part of information from the BLS.

Freelancers usually charge by the project and the most pressing question you normally hear is "how much do I charge?" Many freelance writers have another source of income that is supplementing their writing income. Some are disabled. Others deal with the challenges of raising young children or caring for an elder with illness.

Whether you are seeking some pocket change or desire the income and lifestyle of the writer, there are writing assignments waiting for you. If you have a laptop, internet connection and the necessary skills, you are ready to take on the "life" of a writer.

Let's get started.

## Search for Your First Project

Your browser is your best friend. Narrow the search by using terms like:

- Get paid to write
- Write articles for money
- Earn money writing
- Blog for Cash
- Write blog posts for money

A word to the wise: NEVER use the word "opportunity" in a search for a home business. You will be opening search returns that are mostly scams. Even if you unsubscribe or "opt out" of the resulting unrelenting emails, you and your contact information - will remain on lists sold to list buyers.

Best wishes for success as you pursue your muse!

~~~~~~~~~~~~~~~~~~~~~~~~~~~~~~~~~~~~~~~~

## Exercises:

1) Re-read this section (Mechanics behind Written Information) and find a sentence that can be written using "then" or "than" or both of them. (Then, the bear sauntered away rather than subject itself to injury as a common trespasser.)

2) What is the definition of an Oxford comma?

3) How many subheadings should appear in a 500-word article? How many paragraphs would you expect to write for this article? (7-8 paragraphs with three subheadings.)

# Other Titles in the "Yes You Can" Series

Bookkeeping and Billing
Creative Crafter
[Freelance Writer](Freelance Writer)
Indoor Gardener
Jobs in Jewelry Design
Rapid Resume Creator
Relative Researcher
Talented Transcriptionist
Teaching and Tutoring
Terrific Tax Preparer
Talkative Translator

***

## More Titles by This Author

[Directory of Paying Markets for Freelance Writers](#)

[State of Grenada: Spice of the Caribbean](#)

The Debt Trap - soon

***

NOTES:

NOTES:

www.ingramcontent.com/pod-product-compliance
Lightning Source LLC
Chambersburg PA
CBHW041619180526
45159CB00002BC/927